# 50 Winter Season Recipes for Home

By: Kelly Johnson

# Table of Contents

- Beef Stew
- Chicken Pot Pie
- Butternut Squash Soup
- Lentil Soup
- Chili
- Shepherd's Pie
- Baked Ziti
- Macaroni and Cheese
- Potato Leek Soup
- Beef Stroganoff
- Creamy Tomato Soup
- Vegetable Curry
- Chicken Noodle Soup
- Spaghetti Carbonara
- Stuffed Bell Peppers
- Chicken Alfredo
- Sweet Potato Chili
- Pork Roast
- Eggplant Parmesan
- Tuna Casserole
- Minestrone Soup
- Chicken and Rice Casserole
- Sausage and Peppers
- Mushroom Risotto
- Beef and Barley Soup
- Creamy Broccoli Soup
- Shepherd's Pie
- Chicken Enchiladas
- Beef Chili
- Sweet Potato Casserole
- Tomato Basil Soup
- Lasagna
- Cornbread and Chili
- Chicken Tortilla Soup
- Beef and Vegetable Stew
- Stuffed Acorn Squash

- Mac and Cheese Bake
- Chicken Pot Roast
- Spicy Lentil Soup
- Garlic Mashed Potatoes
- Seafood Chowder
- Baked Chicken Parmesan
- Pork Schnitzel
- Creamy Chicken and Spinach Pasta
- Pot Pie with Biscuits
- Broccoli Cheddar Soup
- Sausage and Kale Soup
- Chicken and Dumplings
- Beef Meatballs in Marinara
- Creamy Shrimp and Grits

**Beef Stew**

**Ingredients:**

- 2 pounds beef chuck, cut into 1-inch cubes
- 3 tablespoons vegetable oil
- 1 large onion, chopped
- 3 cloves garlic, minced
- 4 cups beef broth
- 1 cup red wine (optional, replace with additional broth if preferred)
- 3 tablespoons tomato paste
- 2 tablespoons Worcestershire sauce
- 1 teaspoon dried thyme
- 2 bay leaves
- 4 large carrots, sliced
- 3 potatoes, peeled and cubed
- 1 cup frozen peas
- Salt and black pepper to taste
- 2 tablespoons all-purpose flour (optional, for thickening)
- 2 tablespoons chopped fresh parsley (for garnish)

**Instructions:**

1. **Brown the Beef**: In a large pot or Dutch oven, heat the vegetable oil over medium-high heat. Add the beef cubes in batches, avoiding overcrowding, and brown them on all sides. Transfer the browned beef to a plate.
2. **Sauté the Aromatics**: In the same pot, add the chopped onion and cook until softened, about 5 minutes. Add the garlic and cook for an additional minute.
3. **Deglaze the Pot**: Stir in the tomato paste and cook for 2 minutes. If using wine, pour it in now, scraping the bottom of the pot to loosen any browned bits. Cook for 2-3 minutes, allowing the wine to reduce slightly.
4. **Add Liquids and Seasonings**: Return the beef to the pot. Add the beef broth, Worcestershire sauce, dried thyme, and bay leaves. Bring to a boil.
5. **Simmer the Stew**: Reduce the heat to low, cover, and simmer for about 1.5 hours, or until the beef is tender.
6. **Add Vegetables**: Add the carrots and potatoes to the pot. Continue to simmer for another 30 minutes, or until the vegetables are tender.
7. **Thicken (Optional)**: If you prefer a thicker stew, mix 2 tablespoons of flour with a little water to make a slurry and stir it into the stew. Simmer for an additional 10 minutes until thickened.
8. **Finish and Serve**: Stir in the frozen peas and cook for another 5 minutes. Season with salt and pepper to taste. Remove the bay leaves. Garnish with chopped parsley before serving.

Enjoy your hearty and comforting beef stew!

**Chicken Pot Pie**

**Ingredients:**

**For the Filling:**

- 2 tablespoons butter
- 1 large onion, chopped
- 2 cloves garlic, minced
- 1 cup carrots, diced
- 1 cup celery, diced
- 1 cup frozen peas
- 2 cups cooked chicken, shredded or diced
- 1/4 cup all-purpose flour
- 1 1/2 cups chicken broth
- 1 cup milk
- 1 teaspoon dried thyme
- 1/2 teaspoon dried rosemary
- Salt and black pepper to taste

**For the Crust:**

- 1 package (14.1 ounces) refrigerated pie crusts (or homemade crust)
- 1 egg, beaten (for egg wash)

**Instructions:**

1. **Prepare the Filling:**
   - In a large skillet or saucepan, melt the butter over medium heat. Add the onion and garlic, and cook until softened, about 3-4 minutes.
   - Add the carrots and celery, and cook for an additional 5 minutes.
   - Stir in the flour and cook for 1-2 minutes to form a roux (thickening agent).
   - Gradually add the chicken broth and milk, stirring continuously to avoid lumps. Cook until the mixture starts to thicken.
   - Add the cooked chicken, peas, thyme, rosemary, salt, and pepper. Stir well and cook for a few more minutes until heated through. Remove from heat.
2. **Assemble the Pie:**
   - Preheat your oven to 425°F (220°C).
   - Roll out one pie crust and fit it into a 9-inch pie plate. Trim any excess crust hanging over the edges.
   - Pour the chicken filling into the pie crust.
   - Roll out the second pie crust and place it over the filling. Trim and crimp the edges to seal. Cut a few small slits in the top crust to allow steam to escape.
   - Brush the top crust with the beaten egg for a golden finish.
3. **Bake:**

- Bake in the preheated oven for 30-35 minutes, or until the crust is golden brown and the filling is bubbly.
    - If the edges of the crust start to brown too quickly, cover them with aluminum foil.
4. **Cool and Serve:**
    - Allow the pie to cool for about 10 minutes before serving. This helps the filling set up a bit.

Enjoy your homemade Chicken Pot Pie!

**Butternut Squash Soup**

**Ingredients:**

- 2 tablespoons olive oil
- 1 large onion, chopped
- 2 cloves garlic, minced
- 1 large butternut squash, peeled, seeded, and cubed
- 4 cups vegetable or chicken broth
- 1 teaspoon ground cumin
- 1/2 teaspoon ground nutmeg
- Salt and black pepper to taste
- 1/2 cup heavy cream or coconut milk (optional)
- Fresh parsley or chives for garnish (optional)

**Instructions:**

1. **Sauté the Aromatics:**
   - Heat olive oil in a large pot over medium heat. Add the onion and cook until softened, about 5 minutes. Stir in garlic and cook for another minute.
2. **Cook the Squash:**
   - Add the cubed butternut squash to the pot and cook for about 5 minutes, stirring occasionally.
3. **Add Broth and Spices:**
   - Pour in the broth and add cumin, nutmeg, salt, and pepper. Bring to a boil, then reduce heat and simmer until the squash is tender, about 20-25 minutes.
4. **Blend the Soup:**
   - Use an immersion blender to puree the soup until smooth, or carefully transfer it to a blender in batches and blend until creamy.
5. **Finish and Serve:**
   - If desired, stir in the heavy cream or coconut milk. Adjust seasoning as needed. Garnish with parsley or chives if desired.

Enjoy your creamy and comforting Butternut Squash Soup!

**Lentil Soup**

**Ingredients:**

- 2 tablespoons olive oil
- 1 large onion, chopped
- 2 cloves garlic, minced
- 2 large carrots, diced
- 2 celery stalks, diced
- 1 cup dried lentils (green or brown), rinsed and drained
- 1 can (14.5 ounces) diced tomatoes
- 4 cups vegetable or chicken broth
- 1 teaspoon ground cumin
- 1 teaspoon dried thyme
- 1 bay leaf
- 1 cup chopped kale or spinach (optional)
- Salt and black pepper to taste
- Lemon wedges (for serving, optional)

**Instructions:**

1. **Sauté the Vegetables:**
    - Heat olive oil in a large pot over medium heat. Add the onion and cook until softened, about 5 minutes. Stir in the garlic, carrots, and celery, and cook for another 5 minutes.
2. **Add Lentils and Spices:**
    - Add the rinsed lentils, diced tomatoes (with their juice), cumin, thyme, and bay leaf. Stir well.
3. **Add Broth and Simmer:**
    - Pour in the broth and bring to a boil. Reduce heat to low, cover, and simmer until lentils are tender, about 30-35 minutes.
4. **Finish the Soup:**
    - If using, stir in the chopped kale or spinach and cook for an additional 5 minutes until wilted. Remove the bay leaf. Adjust seasoning with salt and pepper to taste.
5. **Serve:**
    - Serve the soup hot with a squeeze of lemon juice, if desired.

Enjoy your warm and nutritious Lentil Soup!

**Chili**

**Ingredients:**

- 2 tablespoons olive oil
- 1 large onion, chopped
- 3 cloves garlic, minced
- 1 pound ground beef or turkey
- 1 green bell pepper, chopped
- 1 red bell pepper, chopped
- 1 can (14.5 ounces) diced tomatoes
- 1 can (15 ounces) kidney beans, drained and rinsed
- 1 can (15 ounces) black beans, drained and rinsed
- 1 cup beef or vegetable broth
- 2 tablespoons tomato paste
- 2 tablespoons chili powder
- 1 teaspoon ground cumin
- 1/2 teaspoon paprika
- 1/2 teaspoon dried oregano
- 1/4 teaspoon cayenne pepper (optional, for heat)
- Salt and black pepper to taste

**Optional Toppings:**

- Shredded cheese
- Sour cream
- Chopped green onions
- Sliced jalapeños
- Fresh cilantro

**Instructions:**

1. **Cook the Meat:**
   - Heat olive oil in a large pot or Dutch oven over medium heat. Add the chopped onion and cook until softened, about 5 minutes. Add garlic and cook for an additional minute.
   - Add the ground beef or turkey and cook until browned, breaking it up with a spoon as it cooks. Drain any excess fat.
2. **Add Vegetables:**
   - Stir in the chopped bell peppers and cook for about 5 minutes until they start to soften.
3. **Add Tomatoes and Beans:**
   - Add the diced tomatoes, kidney beans, black beans, and beef or vegetable broth. Stir in the tomato paste.
4. **Season and Simmer:**

- Add chili powder, cumin, paprika, oregano, cayenne pepper (if using), salt, and black pepper. Stir well to combine.
- Bring to a boil, then reduce heat to low and simmer uncovered for 30-40 minutes, stirring occasionally. The chili should thicken and the flavors meld together.
5. **Adjust Seasoning:**
    - Taste and adjust seasoning as needed.
6. **Serve:**
    - Ladle the chili into bowls and add your favorite toppings if desired.

Enjoy your hearty and delicious chili!

**Shepherd's Pie**

**Ingredients:**

**For the Filling:**

- 2 tablespoons olive oil
- 1 large onion, chopped
- 2 cloves garlic, minced
- 1 pound ground lamb or beef
- 1 cup carrots, diced
- 1 cup peas
- 1 cup corn (optional)
- 2 tablespoons all-purpose flour
- 1 cup beef or chicken broth
- 1 tablespoon Worcestershire sauce
- 1 teaspoon dried thyme
- Salt and black pepper to taste

**For the Mashed Potatoes:**

- 4 large potatoes, peeled and cubed
- 4 tablespoons butter
- 1/2 cup milk
- Salt and black pepper to taste

**Instructions:**

1. **Prepare the Mashed Potatoes:**
   - Boil the potatoes in salted water until tender, about 15-20 minutes. Drain and return to the pot.
   - Mash the potatoes with butter and milk until smooth. Season with salt and pepper. Set aside.
2. **Make the Filling:**
   - Heat olive oil in a large skillet over medium heat. Add the onion and cook until softened, about 5 minutes. Add garlic and cook for another minute.
   - Add the ground lamb or beef and cook until browned. Drain excess fat if needed.
   - Stir in the carrots and cook for about 5 minutes.
   - Sprinkle the flour over the meat and vegetables, stirring to combine. Cook for 2 minutes.
   - Add the broth, Worcestershire sauce, thyme, salt, and pepper. Stir and simmer until the mixture thickens, about 5-7 minutes.
   - Stir in the peas and corn, if using, and cook for another 2 minutes.
3. **Assemble the Pie:**
   - Preheat your oven to 400°F (200°C).

- Spread the meat filling in an even layer in a baking dish.
- Spoon the mashed potatoes over the filling, spreading them out evenly. Use a fork to create a pattern on top.
4. **Bake:**
    - Bake in the preheated oven for 20-25 minutes, or until the top is golden brown and the filling is bubbling.
5. **Serve:**
    - Let the pie cool for a few minutes before serving.

Enjoy your comforting Shepherd's Pie!

**Baked Ziti**

**Ingredients:**

- 1 pound ziti pasta
- 2 tablespoons olive oil
- 1 large onion, chopped
- 3 cloves garlic, minced
- 1 pound ground beef or Italian sausage
- 2 cups marinara sauce
- 1 can (15 ounces) tomato sauce
- 1 can (6 ounces) tomato paste
- 1 teaspoon dried basil
- 1 teaspoon dried oregano
- 1/2 teaspoon red pepper flakes (optional)
- Salt and black pepper to taste
- 1 cup ricotta cheese
- 1 cup shredded mozzarella cheese
- 1/2 cup grated Parmesan cheese
- Fresh basil or parsley for garnish (optional)

**Instructions:**

1. **Cook the Pasta:**
   - Preheat your oven to 375°F (190°C).
   - Cook the ziti according to package instructions until al dente. Drain and set aside.
2. **Prepare the Meat Sauce:**
   - Heat olive oil in a large skillet over medium heat. Add the onion and cook until softened, about 5 minutes. Add garlic and cook for another minute.
   - Add the ground beef or sausage and cook until browned. Drain excess fat if needed.
   - Stir in the marinara sauce, tomato sauce, tomato paste, basil, oregano, red pepper flakes (if using), salt, and pepper. Simmer for 10 minutes.
3. **Mix Pasta and Cheese:**
   - In a large bowl, combine the cooked ziti with the meat sauce. Stir in the ricotta cheese until well combined.
4. **Assemble the Dish:**
   - Spread half of the ziti mixture in a 9x13-inch baking dish. Sprinkle with half of the mozzarella cheese and Parmesan cheese.
   - Add the remaining ziti mixture on top and sprinkle with the remaining mozzarella and Parmesan cheese.
5. **Bake:**
   - Cover with aluminum foil and bake in the preheated oven for 20 minutes. Remove the foil and bake for an additional 10-15 minutes, or until the cheese is melted and bubbly.

6. **Garnish and Serve:**
    - Let the baked ziti cool for a few minutes before serving. Garnish with fresh basil or parsley if desired.

Enjoy your hearty and comforting Baked Ziti!

**Macaroni and Cheese**

**Ingredients:**

- 8 ounces elbow macaroni
- 2 tablespoons butter
- 2 tablespoons all-purpose flour
- 2 cups milk (whole or 2%)
- 1 cup heavy cream (optional, for extra creaminess)
- 2 cups shredded sharp cheddar cheese
- 1 cup shredded mozzarella cheese
- 1/2 teaspoon salt
- 1/2 teaspoon black pepper
- 1/2 teaspoon paprika
- 1/4 teaspoon garlic powder
- 1/4 teaspoon onion powder
- 1/2 cup grated Parmesan cheese
- 1/2 cup breadcrumbs (for topping)
- 2 tablespoons melted butter (for topping)

**Instructions:**

1. **Cook the Pasta:**
    - Preheat your oven to 350°F (175°C).
    - Cook the macaroni according to package instructions until al dente. Drain and set aside.
2. **Prepare the Cheese Sauce:**
    - In a large saucepan, melt 2 tablespoons of butter over medium heat.
    - Stir in the flour and cook for about 1-2 minutes to form a roux (thickening agent).
    - Gradually whisk in the milk and heavy cream (if using). Continue to whisk until the mixture is smooth and starts to thicken, about 5 minutes.
    - Reduce heat to low and stir in the cheddar and mozzarella cheeses until melted and smooth. Season with salt, pepper, paprika, garlic powder, and onion powder.
3. **Combine Pasta and Cheese Sauce:**
    - Add the cooked macaroni to the cheese sauce and stir to coat the pasta evenly.
4. **Assemble the Dish:**
    - Pour the macaroni and cheese mixture into a greased 9x13-inch baking dish.
    - Sprinkle the grated Parmesan cheese evenly over the top.
5. **Add Topping:**
    - In a small bowl, combine the breadcrumbs with the melted butter. Sprinkle the breadcrumb mixture evenly over the top of the macaroni and cheese.
6. **Bake:**
    - Bake in the preheated oven for 20-25 minutes, or until the top is golden brown and the cheese is bubbly.
7. **Serve:**
    - Allow the macaroni and cheese to cool for a few minutes before serving.

Enjoy your creamy, cheesy macaroni and cheese!

**Potato Leek Soup**

**Ingredients:**

- 2 tablespoons olive oil or butter
- 2 large leeks (white and light green parts only), cleaned and sliced
- 2 cloves garlic, minced
- 4 cups peeled and diced potatoes (about 4 medium potatoes)
- 4 cups vegetable or chicken broth
- 1 cup milk or heavy cream
- 1 teaspoon dried thyme
- Salt and black pepper to taste
- Fresh chives or parsley for garnish (optional)

**Instructions:**

1. **Sauté the Leeks and Garlic:**
   - Heat the olive oil or butter in a large pot over medium heat. Add the leeks and cook until softened, about 5 minutes. Add garlic and cook for an additional minute.
2. **Add Potatoes and Broth:**
   - Stir in the diced potatoes and cook for 2 minutes. Add the broth and thyme. Bring to a boil, then reduce heat and simmer until the potatoes are tender, about 20 minutes.
3. **Blend the Soup:**
   - Use an immersion blender to puree the soup until smooth, or carefully transfer to a blender in batches and blend until creamy.
4. **Finish the Soup:**
   - Stir in the milk or heavy cream and heat through. Season with salt and pepper to taste.
5. **Serve:**
   - Ladle the soup into bowls and garnish with fresh chives or parsley if desired.

Enjoy your creamy and delicious Potato Leek Soup!

**Beef Stroganoff**

**Ingredients:**

- 1 pound beef sirloin or tenderloin, sliced into thin strips
- 2 tablespoons olive oil or butter
- 1 large onion, chopped
- 2 cloves garlic, minced
- 1 cup mushrooms, sliced
- 1 tablespoon all-purpose flour
- 1 cup beef broth
- 1 tablespoon Worcestershire sauce
- 1 teaspoon Dijon mustard
- 1/2 cup sour cream
- Salt and black pepper to taste
- 2 tablespoons chopped fresh parsley (optional, for garnish)

**Instructions:**

1. **Cook the Beef:**
   - Heat olive oil or butter in a large skillet over medium-high heat. Add the beef strips and cook until browned, about 3-4 minutes per side. Remove the beef and set aside.
2. **Sauté Vegetables:**
   - In the same skillet, add the chopped onion and cook until softened, about 5 minutes. Add garlic and cook for another minute. Stir in the mushrooms and cook until they release their moisture and become golden, about 5 minutes.
3. **Make the Sauce:**
   - Sprinkle the flour over the vegetables and stir to combine. Cook for 1-2 minutes.
   - Gradually add the beef broth, Worcestershire sauce, and Dijon mustard, stirring continuously until the mixture thickens.
4. **Combine and Finish:**
   - Return the beef to the skillet and simmer for 5 minutes, or until the beef is cooked through and the sauce is well combined.
   - Stir in the sour cream and heat through, but do not boil. Season with salt and pepper to taste.
5. **Serve:**
   - Garnish with chopped parsley if desired. Serve over egg noodles, rice, or mashed potatoes.

Enjoy your rich and creamy Beef Stroganoff!

**Creamy Tomato Soup**

**Ingredients:**

- 2 tablespoons olive oil or butter
- 1 large onion, chopped
- 3 cloves garlic, minced
- 2 cans (14.5 ounces each) diced tomatoes (or about 4 cups fresh tomatoes, peeled and chopped)
- 1 cup chicken or vegetable broth
- 1 teaspoon dried basil
- 1 teaspoon dried oregano
- 1/2 teaspoon sugar (optional, to balance acidity)
- 1 cup heavy cream or whole milk
- Salt and black pepper to taste
- Fresh basil or parsley for garnish (optional)

**Instructions:**

1. **Sauté the Aromatics:**
   - Heat olive oil or butter in a large pot over medium heat. Add the chopped onion and cook until softened and translucent, about 5 minutes. Stir in the garlic and cook for an additional minute.
2. **Add Tomatoes and Broth:**
   - Add the diced tomatoes (with their juice) and the chicken or vegetable broth to the pot. Stir in the dried basil, oregano, and sugar (if using).
3. **Simmer:**
   - Bring the mixture to a boil, then reduce the heat and simmer for 15-20 minutes to allow the flavors to meld together.
4. **Blend the Soup:**
   - Use an immersion blender to puree the soup until smooth, or carefully transfer it to a blender in batches and blend until creamy.
5. **Add Cream and Season:**
   - Return the blended soup to the pot. Stir in the heavy cream or milk and heat through. Season with salt and pepper to taste.
6. **Serve:**
   - Ladle the soup into bowls and garnish with fresh basil or parsley if desired.

Enjoy your comforting and creamy tomato soup!

**Vegetable Curry**

**Ingredients:**

- 2 tablespoons vegetable oil
- 1 large onion, chopped
- 3 cloves garlic, minced
- 1 tablespoon fresh ginger, minced
- 2 tablespoons curry powder
- 1 teaspoon ground cumin
- 1 teaspoon turmeric
- 1/2 teaspoon paprika
- 1 can (14.5 ounces) diced tomatoes
- 1 cup vegetable broth
- 1 cup coconut milk
- 2 cups mixed vegetables (e.g., carrots, bell peppers, potatoes, peas, cauliflower), chopped
- 1 cup spinach or kale (optional)
- Salt and black pepper to taste
- Fresh cilantro for garnish (optional)

**Instructions:**

1. **Sauté Aromatics:**
    - Heat vegetable oil in a large pot over medium heat. Add the chopped onion and cook until softened, about 5 minutes. Stir in the garlic and ginger and cook for another minute.
2. **Add Spices:**
    - Add curry powder, cumin, turmeric, and paprika. Cook for 1-2 minutes, stirring constantly to release the flavors.
3. **Add Tomatoes and Broth:**
    - Stir in the diced tomatoes, vegetable broth, and coconut milk. Bring to a simmer.
4. **Add Vegetables:**
    - Add the chopped vegetables and cook until tender, about 15-20 minutes. If using, stir in the spinach or kale and cook for another 5 minutes until wilted.
5. **Season and Serve:**
    - Season with salt and pepper to taste. Garnish with fresh cilantro if desired.

Enjoy your hearty and aromatic Vegetable Curry!

**Chicken Noodle Soup**

**Ingredients:**

- 2 tablespoons olive oil or butter
- 1 large onion, chopped
- 2 cloves garlic, minced
- 3 large carrots, sliced
- 2 celery stalks, sliced
- 1 teaspoon dried thyme
- 1 teaspoon dried rosemary
- 1 bay leaf
- 6 cups chicken broth
- 2 cups cooked chicken, shredded or diced (rotisserie chicken works well)
- 1 1/2 cups egg noodles or pasta of your choice
- Salt and black pepper to taste
- Fresh parsley for garnish (optional)

**Instructions:**

1. **Sauté Vegetables:**
   - Heat olive oil or butter in a large pot over medium heat. Add the chopped onion and cook until softened, about 5 minutes. Stir in the garlic and cook for an additional minute.
2. **Add Carrots and Celery:**
   - Add the sliced carrots and celery to the pot. Cook for about 5 minutes, stirring occasionally.
3. **Add Broth and Herbs:**
   - Stir in the dried thyme, dried rosemary, and bay leaf. Add the chicken broth and bring to a boil.
4. **Simmer:**
   - Reduce the heat and let the soup simmer for about 10 minutes, or until the carrots and celery are tender.
5. **Add Chicken and Noodles:**
   - Add the cooked chicken and noodles to the pot. Continue to simmer until the noodles are cooked through, about 8-10 minutes.
6. **Season and Serve:**
   - Season with salt and black pepper to taste. Remove the bay leaf before serving.
   - Garnish with fresh parsley if desired.

Enjoy your warm and comforting Chicken Noodle Soup!


**Spaghetti Carbonara**

**Ingredients:**

- 12 ounces spaghetti
- 2 tablespoons olive oil
- 4 ounces pancetta or guanciale, diced
- 2 cloves garlic, minced
- 3 large eggs
- 1 cup grated Parmesan cheese
- 1/2 cup heavy cream (optional, for extra creaminess)
- Salt and black pepper to taste
- Fresh parsley, chopped (optional, for garnish)

**Instructions:**

1. **Cook the Pasta:**
    - Cook the spaghetti according to package instructions until al dente. Reserve 1 cup of pasta cooking water before draining.
2. **Cook Pancetta:**
    - Heat olive oil in a large skillet over medium heat. Add the diced pancetta and cook until crispy, about 5-7 minutes. Remove from heat and stir in the minced garlic, letting it cook briefly with residual heat.
3. **Prepare Sauce:**
    - In a bowl, whisk together the eggs, Parmesan cheese, and heavy cream (if using). Season with a pinch of black pepper.
4. **Combine Pasta and Sauce:**
    - Add the drained spaghetti to the skillet with pancetta. Toss to combine and cool slightly to avoid scrambling the eggs.
    - Pour the egg mixture over the pasta, tossing quickly to coat and create a creamy sauce. Add a bit of reserved pasta water if needed to achieve the desired consistency.
5. **Season and Serve:**
    - Season with additional salt and pepper to taste. Garnish with fresh parsley if desired.

Enjoy your creamy and savory Spaghetti Carbonara!

**Stuffed Bell Peppers**

**Ingredients:**

- 4 large bell peppers (any color)
- 1 tablespoon olive oil
- 1 onion, chopped
- 2 cloves garlic, minced
- 1 pound ground beef or turkey
- 1 cup cooked rice (white, brown, or jasmine)
- 1 can (14.5 ounces) diced tomatoes
- 1 cup shredded cheese (cheddar, mozzarella, or your choice)
- 1 teaspoon dried oregano
- 1 teaspoon dried basil
- Salt and black pepper to taste
- Fresh parsley or basil for garnish (optional)

**Instructions:**

1. **Preheat the Oven:**
    - Preheat your oven to 375°F (190°C).
2. **Prepare the Peppers:**
    - Cut the tops off the bell peppers and remove the seeds and membranes. Set aside.
3. **Cook the Filling:**
    - Heat olive oil in a large skillet over medium heat. Add the chopped onion and cook until softened, about 5 minutes. Add garlic and cook for another minute.
    - Add the ground beef or turkey and cook until browned. Drain any excess fat.
    - Stir in the cooked rice, diced tomatoes (with their juice), oregano, basil, salt, and pepper. Cook for another 5 minutes until heated through.
4. **Stuff the Peppers:**
    - Spoon the filling mixture into each bell pepper, packing it in lightly. Place the stuffed peppers upright in a baking dish.
5. **Bake:**
    - Top each pepper with shredded cheese. Cover the baking dish with aluminum foil.
    - Bake in the preheated oven for 30 minutes. Remove the foil and bake for an additional 10 minutes, or until the peppers are tender and the cheese is melted and bubbly.
6. **Garnish and Serve:**
    - Garnish with fresh parsley or basil if desired. Serve hot.

Enjoy your hearty and flavorful Stuffed Bell Peppers!

**Chicken Alfredo**

**Ingredients:**

- 2 tablespoons olive oil
- 2 boneless, skinless chicken breasts
- Salt and black pepper to taste
- 1/2 teaspoon garlic powder
- 1/2 teaspoon Italian seasoning (optional)
- 8 ounces fettuccine pasta
- 2 tablespoons butter
- 2 cloves garlic, minced
- 1 cup heavy cream
- 1 cup grated Parmesan cheese
- 1/4 cup chopped fresh parsley (optional, for garnish)

**Instructions:**

1. **Cook the Chicken:**
   - Heat olive oil in a skillet over medium heat. Season the chicken breasts with salt, pepper, garlic powder, and Italian seasoning.
   - Cook the chicken for 6-7 minutes per side until fully cooked and golden brown. Remove from the skillet and let rest before slicing into strips.
2. **Cook the Pasta:**
   - Cook fettuccine according to package instructions until al dente. Drain and set aside.
3. **Make the Alfredo Sauce:**
   - In the same skillet used for the chicken, melt the butter over medium heat. Add the minced garlic and cook for about 1 minute until fragrant.
   - Stir in the heavy cream and bring to a simmer. Cook for 2-3 minutes, stirring occasionally.
   - Gradually whisk in the Parmesan cheese until the sauce is smooth and thickened. Season with salt and pepper to taste.
4. **Combine:**
   - Toss the cooked fettuccine in the Alfredo sauce until well coated. Add the sliced chicken on top.
5. **Serve:**
   - Garnish with fresh parsley if desired. Serve hot.

Enjoy your rich and creamy Chicken Alfredo!

**Sweet Potato Chili**

## Ingredients:

- 2 tablespoons olive oil
- 1 large onion, chopped
- 2 cloves garlic, minced
- 1 pound ground beef or turkey
- 2 large sweet potatoes, peeled and diced
- 1 can (14.5 ounces) diced tomatoes
- 1 can (15 ounces) kidney beans, drained and rinsed
- 1 can (15 ounces) black beans, drained and rinsed
- 1 cup vegetable or chicken broth
- 2 tablespoons chili powder
- 1 teaspoon ground cumin
- 1 teaspoon smoked paprika
- 1/2 teaspoon ground cinnamon (optional)
- Salt and black pepper to taste
- 1 cup corn kernels (fresh, frozen, or canned)
- Fresh cilantro or chopped green onions for garnish (optional)

## Instructions:

1. **Cook the Meat:**
   - Heat olive oil in a large pot over medium heat. Add the onion and cook until softened, about 5 minutes. Stir in the garlic and cook for another minute.
   - Add the ground beef or turkey and cook until browned. Drain any excess fat if necessary.
2. **Add Sweet Potatoes and Spices:**
   - Stir in the diced sweet potatoes, chili powder, cumin, smoked paprika, and cinnamon (if using). Cook for about 2 minutes, allowing the spices to coat the sweet potatoes.
3. **Add Tomatoes and Beans:**
   - Stir in the diced tomatoes, kidney beans, black beans, and broth. Bring to a boil, then reduce heat to a simmer.
4. **Simmer:**
   - Cover and simmer for about 25-30 minutes, or until the sweet potatoes are tender and the chili has thickened.
5. **Add Corn and Final Touches:**
   - Stir in the corn and cook for an additional 5 minutes. Season with salt and pepper to taste.
6. **Serve:**
   - Garnish with fresh cilantro or chopped green onions if desired. Serve hot.

Enjoy your flavorful and nutritious Sweet Potato Chili!

**Pork Roast**

**Ingredients:**

- 3-4 pound pork shoulder or pork loin
- 2 tablespoons olive oil
- 4 cloves garlic, minced
- 1 tablespoon fresh rosemary, chopped (or 1 teaspoon dried rosemary)
- 1 tablespoon fresh thyme, chopped (or 1 teaspoon dried thyme)
- 1 teaspoon salt
- 1/2 teaspoon black pepper
- 1/2 teaspoon paprika
- 1 cup chicken or vegetable broth
- 1 cup white wine or additional broth (optional)
- 1 large onion, quartered
- 2 carrots, peeled and cut into chunks
- 2 celery stalks, cut into chunks

**Instructions:**

1. **Preheat the Oven:**
    - Preheat your oven to 375°F (190°C).
2. **Prepare the Pork:**
    - Rub the pork roast with olive oil. In a small bowl, mix together garlic, rosemary, thyme, salt, pepper, and paprika. Rub this mixture all over the pork.
3. **Sear the Pork:**
    - Heat a large oven-safe skillet or Dutch oven over medium-high heat. Sear the pork roast on all sides until browned, about 3-4 minutes per side.
4. **Add Vegetables and Liquid:**
    - Add the onion, carrots, and celery around the pork in the skillet. Pour the broth and white wine (if using) over the roast and vegetables.
5. **Roast:**
    - Transfer the skillet to the preheated oven and roast for about 1.5 to 2 hours, or until the pork reaches an internal temperature of 145°F (63°C) and is tender. Baste occasionally with the pan juices.
6. **Rest and Serve:**
    - Remove the pork from the oven and let it rest for 10-15 minutes before slicing. Serve with the roasted vegetables and pan juices.

Enjoy your flavorful and tender Pork Roast!

**Eggplant Parmesan**

**Ingredients:**

- 2 large eggplants, sliced into 1/4-inch rounds
- Salt
- 1 cup all-purpose flour
- 2 large eggs, beaten
- 2 cups breadcrumbs (Italian or plain)
- 1 cup grated Parmesan cheese
- 2 cups marinara sauce
- 2 cups shredded mozzarella cheese
- 1/2 cup fresh basil leaves (optional, for garnish)
- Olive oil for frying

**Instructions:**

1. **Prepare Eggplant:**
   - Preheat your oven to 375°F (190°C).
   - Arrange the eggplant slices on a baking sheet and sprinkle with salt. Let sit for 30 minutes to draw out excess moisture. Rinse and pat dry with paper towels.
2. **Bread the Eggplant:**
   - Set up a breading station: one plate with flour, one with beaten eggs, and one with breadcrumbs mixed with 1/2 cup Parmesan cheese.
   - Dredge each eggplant slice in flour, dip in beaten eggs, and coat with breadcrumbs.
3. **Fry the Eggplant:**
   - Heat olive oil in a large skillet over medium heat. Fry the eggplant slices in batches until golden brown on both sides, about 3-4 minutes per side. Drain on paper towels.
4. **Assemble the Dish:**
   - Spread a thin layer of marinara sauce on the bottom of a baking dish. Arrange a layer of fried eggplant slices over the sauce. Top with more marinara sauce, a sprinkle of Parmesan cheese, and a layer of mozzarella cheese.
   - Repeat layers until all ingredients are used, ending with a layer of cheese.
5. **Bake:**
   - Bake in the preheated oven for 25-30 minutes, or until the cheese is melted and bubbly, and the eggplant is tender.
6. **Garnish and Serve:**
   - Let the dish cool slightly before serving. Garnish with fresh basil if desired.

Enjoy your delicious and comforting Eggplant Parmesan!


**Tuna Casserole**

**Ingredients:**

- 8 ounces egg noodles
- 2 tablespoons olive oil or butter
- 1 small onion, chopped
- 2 cloves garlic, minced
- 1 can (15 ounces) tuna, drained and flaked
- 1 cup frozen peas (or fresh if preferred)
- 1 can (10.5 ounces) cream of mushroom soup
- 1 cup milk
- 1 cup shredded cheddar cheese
- 1/2 teaspoon dried thyme
- Salt and black pepper to taste
- 1/2 cup breadcrumbs (optional, for topping)
- 2 tablespoons melted butter (optional, for topping)

**Instructions:**

1. **Preheat the Oven:**
   - Preheat your oven to 375°F (190°C).
2. **Cook the Noodles:**
   - Cook the egg noodles according to package instructions until al dente. Drain and set aside.
3. **Prepare the Casserole Base:**
   - Heat olive oil or butter in a large skillet over medium heat. Add the chopped onion and cook until softened, about 5 minutes. Stir in the garlic and cook for another minute.
   - Add the flaked tuna and peas. Cook for 2-3 minutes until heated through.
4. **Make the Sauce:**
   - In a large bowl, mix together the cream of mushroom soup, milk, cheddar cheese, dried thyme, salt, and pepper. Add the cooked noodles and tuna mixture, stirring to combine.
5. **Assemble the Casserole:**
   - Transfer the mixture to a greased 9x13-inch baking dish.
6. **Add Topping:**
   - If using, mix the breadcrumbs with melted butter and sprinkle evenly over the casserole.
7. **Bake:**
   - Bake in the preheated oven for 20-25 minutes, or until the casserole is bubbly and the topping is golden brown.
8. **Serve:**
   - Allow the casserole to cool for a few minutes before serving.

Enjoy your comforting and hearty Tuna Casserole!

**Minestrone Soup**

**Ingredients:**

- 2 tablespoons olive oil
- 1 large onion, chopped
- 2 cloves garlic, minced
- 2 carrots, diced
- 2 celery stalks, diced
- 1 zucchini, diced
- 1 cup green beans, chopped
- 1 cup potatoes, diced
- 1 can (14.5 ounces) diced tomatoes
- 4 cups vegetable or chicken broth
- 1 can (15 ounces) kidney beans, drained and rinsed
- 1 cup pasta (small shapes like ditalini or elbow)
- 1 teaspoon dried basil
- 1 teaspoon dried oregano
- Salt and black pepper to taste
- 2 cups fresh spinach or kale
- 1/4 cup grated Parmesan cheese (optional, for serving)

**Instructions:**

1. **Sauté Vegetables:**
   - Heat olive oil in a large pot over medium heat. Add the onion and cook until softened, about 5 minutes. Stir in the garlic and cook for an additional minute.
   - Add carrots and celery, cooking for another 5 minutes until they start to soften.
2. **Add Remaining Vegetables:**
   - Stir in zucchini, green beans, and potatoes. Cook for a few minutes.
3. **Add Broth and Tomatoes:**
   - Pour in the diced tomatoes and broth. Bring to a boil, then reduce heat and simmer for 15 minutes.
4. **Add Beans and Pasta:**
   - Stir in the kidney beans, pasta, basil, oregano, salt, and pepper. Continue to simmer until the pasta and vegetables are tender, about 10-12 minutes.
5. **Finish and Serve:**
   - Stir in the fresh spinach or kale and cook until wilted, about 2 minutes. Adjust seasoning as needed.
   - Serve hot, optionally topped with grated Parmesan cheese.

Enjoy your flavorful and nourishing Minestrone Soup!


**Chicken and Rice Casserole**

**Ingredients:**

- 2 tablespoons olive oil or butter
- 1 onion, chopped
- 2 cloves garlic, minced
- 1 cup long-grain white rice (uncooked)
- 2 cups chicken broth
- 1 cup milk
- 1 can (10.5 ounces) cream of chicken soup
- 2 cups cooked chicken, shredded or diced (rotisserie chicken works well)
- 1 cup frozen peas and carrots mix
- 1 cup shredded cheddar cheese
- 1/2 teaspoon dried thyme
- Salt and black pepper to taste
- 1/2 cup breadcrumbs (optional, for topping)
- 2 tablespoons melted butter (optional, for topping)

**Instructions:**

1. **Preheat the Oven:**
   - Preheat your oven to 375°F (190°C).
2. **Sauté Aromatics:**
   - Heat olive oil or butter in a large skillet over medium heat. Add the chopped onion and cook until softened, about 5 minutes. Stir in the garlic and cook for an additional minute.
3. **Combine Ingredients:**
   - In a large bowl, mix together the uncooked rice, chicken broth, milk, cream of chicken soup, cooked chicken, frozen peas and carrots, and half of the shredded cheddar cheese. Stir in the sautéed onions and garlic. Season with thyme, salt, and pepper.
4. **Assemble the Casserole:**
   - Pour the mixture into a greased 9x13-inch baking dish. Spread evenly and top with the remaining cheese.
5. **Add Topping (Optional):**
   - Mix the breadcrumbs with melted butter and sprinkle evenly over the casserole if using.
6. **Bake:**
   - Bake in the preheated oven for 30-35 minutes, or until the casserole is bubbly and the top is golden brown.
7. **Serve:**
   - Let the casserole cool slightly before serving.

Enjoy your creamy and satisfying Chicken and Rice Casserole!

**Sausage and Peppers**

**Ingredients:**

- 2 tablespoons olive oil
- 1 pound Italian sausage (sweet or hot, based on preference)
- 1 large onion, sliced
- 2 red bell peppers, sliced
- 2 green bell peppers, sliced
- 2 cloves garlic, minced
- 1 can (14.5 ounces) diced tomatoes (optional, for a saucier dish)
- 1 teaspoon dried oregano
- 1 teaspoon dried basil
- Salt and black pepper to taste
- Fresh parsley or basil for garnish (optional)

**Instructions:**

1. **Cook the Sausage:**
   - Heat olive oil in a large skillet over medium heat. Add the sausage links and cook until browned on all sides and cooked through, about 10-12 minutes. Remove from the skillet and set aside.
2. **Sauté Vegetables:**
   - In the same skillet, add the sliced onion and bell peppers. Cook until they begin to soften, about 5-7 minutes. Stir in the garlic and cook for another minute.
3. **Add Tomatoes and Seasonings:**
   - If using, stir in the diced tomatoes. Add oregano, basil, salt, and pepper. Cook for an additional 5 minutes.
4. **Combine and Serve:**
   - Slice the cooked sausage into bite-sized pieces and return to the skillet. Stir to combine and heat through for another 5 minutes.
5. **Garnish and Serve:**
   - Garnish with fresh parsley or basil if desired. Serve hot.

Enjoy your flavorful Sausage and Peppers dish!

**Mushroom Risotto**

**Ingredients:**

- 2 tablespoons olive oil or butter
- 1 small onion, finely chopped
- 2 cloves garlic, minced
- 1 cup Arborio rice
- 1 cup dry white wine
- 4 cups chicken or vegetable broth, kept warm
- 1 cup mushrooms (cremini, shiitake, or a mix), sliced
- 1/2 cup grated Parmesan cheese
- 2 tablespoons chopped fresh parsley (optional, for garnish)
- Salt and black pepper to taste

**Instructions:**

1. **Prepare the Broth:**
   - Keep the broth warm in a saucepan over low heat.
2. **Sauté Mushrooms:**
   - In a large skillet or pot, heat olive oil or butter over medium heat. Add the sliced mushrooms and cook until browned and tender, about 5-7 minutes. Remove and set aside.
3. **Cook Aromatics:**
   - In the same skillet, add a little more oil or butter if needed. Sauté the onion until translucent, about 5 minutes. Stir in the garlic and cook for another minute.
4. **Add Rice:**
   - Add the Arborio rice and cook, stirring frequently, for 2-3 minutes until the edges become translucent.
5. **Deglaze with Wine:**
   - Pour in the white wine and cook, stirring, until it is mostly absorbed by the rice.
6. **Add Broth:**
   - Begin adding the warm broth one ladleful at a time, stirring frequently and allowing each addition to be absorbed before adding more. Continue until the rice is creamy and cooked to al dente, about 18-20 minutes.
7. **Finish the Risotto:**
   - Stir in the cooked mushrooms and Parmesan cheese. Season with salt and pepper to taste. Garnish with fresh parsley if desired.
8. **Serve:**
   - Serve the risotto hot.

Enjoy your rich and creamy Mushroom Risotto!


**Beef and Barley Soup**

**Ingredients:**

- 2 tablespoons olive oil
- 1 pound beef stew meat, cut into cubes
- 1 large onion, chopped
- 2 cloves garlic, minced
- 2 carrots, diced
- 2 celery stalks, diced
- 1 cup pearl barley
- 1 can (14.5 ounces) diced tomatoes
- 6 cups beef broth
- 1 bay leaf
- 1 teaspoon dried thyme
- Salt and black pepper to taste
- 1 cup frozen peas or green beans (optional)
- 2 tablespoons chopped fresh parsley (optional, for garnish)

**Instructions:**

1. **Brown the Beef:**
    - Heat olive oil in a large pot over medium-high heat. Add the beef cubes and brown on all sides. Remove beef from the pot and set aside.
2. **Sauté Vegetables:**
    - In the same pot, add the onion, carrots, and celery. Cook until the vegetables are softened, about 5 minutes. Stir in the garlic and cook for another minute.
3. **Add Barley and Liquid:**
    - Return the beef to the pot. Stir in the pearl barley, diced tomatoes, beef broth, bay leaf, and dried thyme.
4. **Simmer:**
    - Bring the soup to a boil, then reduce heat and let it simmer, covered, for about 1 to 1.5 hours, or until the beef and barley are tender. Stir occasionally.
5. **Add Final Ingredients:**
    - If using, stir in the frozen peas or green beans and cook for an additional 5-10 minutes. Season with salt and pepper to taste.
6. **Garnish and Serve:**
    - Remove the bay leaf before serving. Garnish with fresh parsley if desired.

Enjoy your hearty and flavorful Beef and Barley Soup!

**Creamy Broccoli Soup**

**Ingredients:**

- 2 tablespoons olive oil or butter
- 1 large onion, chopped
- 2 cloves garlic, minced
- 4 cups broccoli florets (about 1 large head)
- 2 cups vegetable or chicken broth
- 1 cup milk or heavy cream
- 1 cup shredded cheddar cheese (optional, for added creaminess)
- 1/2 teaspoon dried thyme
- Salt and black pepper to taste
- Fresh parsley for garnish (optional)

**Instructions:**

1. **Sauté Aromatics:**
   - Heat olive oil or butter in a large pot over medium heat. Add the chopped onion and cook until softened, about 5 minutes. Stir in the garlic and cook for another minute.
2. **Cook Broccoli:**
   - Add the broccoli florets and cook for 5 minutes, stirring occasionally.
3. **Add Broth:**
   - Pour in the vegetable or chicken broth. Bring to a boil, then reduce heat and simmer for about 10-15 minutes, or until the broccoli is tender.
4. **Blend the Soup:**
   - Use an immersion blender to puree the soup until smooth, or carefully transfer to a blender in batches and blend until creamy.
5. **Add Cream and Cheese:**
   - Return the soup to the pot if needed. Stir in the milk or heavy cream and shredded cheddar cheese (if using). Heat through until the cheese is melted and the soup is creamy. Season with thyme, salt, and pepper.
6. **Serve:**
   - Garnish with fresh parsley if desired. Serve hot.

Enjoy your creamy and comforting Broccoli Soup!

**Shepherd's Pie**

**Ingredients:**

**For the Filling:**

- 2 tablespoons olive oil
- 1 large onion, chopped
- 2 cloves garlic, minced
- 1 pound ground beef or lamb
- 2 carrots, diced
- 2 celery stalks, diced
- 1 cup frozen peas
- 2 tablespoons tomato paste
- 1 tablespoon Worcestershire sauce
- 1 teaspoon dried thyme
- 1 teaspoon dried rosemary
- 1/2 cup beef broth
- Salt and black pepper to taste

**For the Mashed Potatoes:**

- 2 pounds potatoes (Russet or Yukon Gold), peeled and diced
- 1/2 cup milk
- 4 tablespoons butter
- Salt and black pepper to taste

**Instructions:**

1. **Prepare the Mashed Potatoes:**
   - Place the diced potatoes in a large pot and cover with water. Bring to a boil and cook until tender, about 15-20 minutes. Drain and return to the pot.
   - Mash the potatoes with milk and butter until smooth and creamy. Season with salt and pepper to taste. Set aside.
2. **Cook the Filling:**
   - Heat olive oil in a large skillet over medium heat. Add the chopped onion and cook until softened, about 5 minutes. Stir in the garlic and cook for another minute.
   - Add the ground beef or lamb and cook until browned. Drain excess fat if necessary.
   - Stir in the carrots and celery and cook for 5 minutes until softened.
   - Add tomato paste, Worcestershire sauce, thyme, rosemary, and beef broth. Simmer for 5-10 minutes until the mixture thickens. Stir in the frozen peas and cook for another 2 minutes. Season with salt and pepper.
3. **Assemble the Pie:**
   - Preheat your oven to 375°F (190°C).

- Transfer the meat mixture to a baking dish (about 9x13 inches). Spread the mashed potatoes evenly over the top, smoothing with a spatula. You can use a fork to create a textured pattern on top if desired.
4. **Bake:**
    - Bake in the preheated oven for 25-30 minutes, or until the top is golden brown and the filling is bubbling.
5. **Serve:**
    - Let the Shepherd's Pie cool slightly before serving.

Enjoy your comforting and classic Shepherd's Pie!

**Chicken Enchiladas**

**Ingredients:**

- 2 tablespoons olive oil
- 1 small onion, chopped
- 2 cloves garlic, minced
- 2 cups cooked chicken, shredded (rotisserie chicken works well)
- 1 can (15 ounces) enchilada sauce (red or green)
- 1 cup sour cream or Greek yogurt
- 1 cup shredded cheddar or Monterey Jack cheese
- 8-10 flour or corn tortillas
- 1 can (4.5 ounces) diced green chilies (optional)
- 1/2 cup chopped fresh cilantro (optional, for garnish)

**Instructions:**

1. **Preheat Oven:**
   - Preheat your oven to 375°F (190°C).
2. **Prepare the Filling:**
   - Heat olive oil in a skillet over medium heat. Add the chopped onion and cook until softened, about 5 minutes. Stir in the garlic and cook for another minute.
   - Add the shredded chicken and mix well. Stir in 1/2 cup of the enchilada sauce and the diced green chilies if using. Cook for another 2-3 minutes.
3. **Assemble the Enchiladas:**
   - Spread a small amount of enchilada sauce in the bottom of a baking dish to prevent sticking.
   - Place a portion of the chicken mixture in each tortilla, sprinkle with cheese, and roll up. Place the filled tortillas seam-side down in the baking dish.
4. **Add Sauce and Cheese:**
   - Pour the remaining enchilada sauce over the tortillas. Sprinkle with the remaining cheese.
5. **Bake:**
   - Bake in the preheated oven for 20-25 minutes, or until the cheese is melted and bubbly, and the enchiladas are heated through.
6. **Serve:**
   - Garnish with fresh cilantro if desired. Serve hot.

Enjoy your flavorful and satisfying Chicken Enchiladas!

**Beef Chili**

**Ingredients:**

- 2 tablespoons olive oil
- 1 pound ground beef
- 1 large onion, chopped
- 2 cloves garlic, minced
- 1 bell pepper, diced (red or green)
- 2 cans (14.5 ounces each) diced tomatoes
- 1 can (15 ounces) kidney beans, drained and rinsed
- 1 can (15 ounces) black beans, drained and rinsed
- 1 cup beef broth
- 2 tablespoons chili powder
- 1 teaspoon ground cumin
- 1 teaspoon smoked paprika
- 1/2 teaspoon cayenne pepper (optional, for heat)
- Salt and black pepper to taste
- 1 cup corn kernels (optional)
- Shredded cheese, sour cream, and chopped green onions for garnish (optional)

**Instructions:**

1. **Cook the Beef:**
   - Heat olive oil in a large pot over medium heat. Add ground beef and cook until browned, breaking it up with a spoon. Drain excess fat if necessary.
2. **Sauté Vegetables:**
   - Add chopped onion, garlic, and bell pepper to the pot. Cook until the vegetables are softened, about 5 minutes.
3. **Add Remaining Ingredients:**
   - Stir in the diced tomatoes, kidney beans, black beans, beef broth, chili powder, cumin, smoked paprika, cayenne pepper (if using), salt, and pepper. Bring to a boil.
4. **Simmer:**
   - Reduce heat and simmer for 20-30 minutes, stirring occasionally. If using, stir in corn kernels and cook for an additional 5 minutes.
5. **Serve:**
   - Garnish with shredded cheese, sour cream, and chopped green onions if desired.

Enjoy your hearty and flavorful Beef Chili!


**Sweet Potato Casserole**

**Ingredients:**

**For the Casserole:**

- 4 cups cooked and mashed sweet potatoes (about 4 medium sweet potatoes)
- 1/2 cup brown sugar
- 1/4 cup butter, melted
- 2 large eggs
- 1/2 cup milk
- 1 teaspoon vanilla extract
- 1/2 teaspoon ground cinnamon
- 1/4 teaspoon ground nutmeg
- Salt to taste

**For the Topping:**

- 1/2 cup brown sugar
- 1/3 cup all-purpose flour
- 1/4 cup butter, cold and cut into small pieces
- 1/2 cup chopped pecans or walnuts (optional)

**Instructions:**

1. **Preheat Oven:**
    - Preheat your oven to 375°F (190°C).
2. **Prepare the Casserole:**
    - In a large bowl, mix together the mashed sweet potatoes, brown sugar, melted butter, eggs, milk, vanilla extract, cinnamon, nutmeg, and salt until well combined.
3. **Assemble the Casserole:**
    - Transfer the sweet potato mixture to a greased 9x13-inch baking dish.
4. **Prepare the Topping:**
    - In a separate bowl, combine brown sugar, flour, and cold butter. Use a fork or pastry cutter to mix until crumbly. Stir in the chopped nuts if using.
5. **Add Topping and Bake:**
    - Sprinkle the topping evenly over the sweet potato mixture.
    - Bake in the preheated oven for 30-35 minutes, or until the topping is golden brown and the casserole is heated through.
6. **Serve:**
    - Let cool slightly before serving.

Enjoy your sweet and comforting Sweet Potato Casserole!

**Tomato Basil Soup**

**Ingredients:**

- 2 tablespoons olive oil
- 1 large onion, chopped
- 2 cloves garlic, minced
- 2 cans (14.5 ounces each) diced tomatoes (or about 4 cups fresh tomatoes, peeled and chopped)
- 2 cups vegetable or chicken broth
- 1 teaspoon sugar (optional, to balance acidity)
- 1/2 teaspoon dried basil or 1 cup fresh basil leaves
- 1/2 cup heavy cream or whole milk
- Salt and black pepper to taste
- Fresh basil leaves for garnish (optional)

**Instructions:**

1. **Sauté Aromatics:**
    - Heat olive oil in a large pot over medium heat. Add the chopped onion and cook until softened, about 5 minutes. Stir in the garlic and cook for another minute.
2. **Add Tomatoes and Broth:**
    - Add the diced tomatoes (with their juice) and vegetable or chicken broth. Stir in the sugar if using. Bring to a boil, then reduce heat and simmer for 15 minutes.
3. **Blend the Soup:**
    - Use an immersion blender to puree the soup until smooth, or carefully transfer the soup in batches to a blender and blend until creamy.
4. **Add Cream and Basil:**
    - Return the soup to the pot if needed. Stir in the heavy cream or milk and fresh basil leaves (if using). Heat through, but do not boil.
5. **Season and Serve:**
    - Season with salt and pepper to taste. Garnish with fresh basil leaves if desired.

Enjoy your rich and flavorful Tomato Basil Soup!

**Lasagna**

**Ingredients:**

**For the Meat Sauce:**

- 2 tablespoons olive oil
- 1 pound ground beef or Italian sausage
- 1 large onion, chopped
- 2 cloves garlic, minced
- 1 can (28 ounces) crushed tomatoes
- 2 tablespoons tomato paste
- 1 teaspoon dried basil
- 1 teaspoon dried oregano
- 1/2 teaspoon sugar (optional, to balance acidity)
- Salt and black pepper to taste

**For the Cheese Mixture:**

- 1 container (15 ounces) ricotta cheese
- 1 egg
- 1 cup grated Parmesan cheese
- 2 cups shredded mozzarella cheese

**Additional Ingredients:**

- 9-12 lasagna noodles (depending on dish size)
- Extra mozzarella cheese for topping

**Instructions:**

1. **Preheat Oven:**
   - Preheat your oven to 375°F (190°C).
2. **Prepare the Meat Sauce:**
   - Heat olive oil in a large skillet over medium heat. Add the ground beef or sausage and cook until browned. Drain excess fat if needed.
   - Add the chopped onion and cook until softened, about 5 minutes. Stir in the garlic and cook for another minute.
   - Add crushed tomatoes, tomato paste, basil, oregano, sugar (if using), salt, and pepper. Simmer for 20 minutes, stirring occasionally.
3. **Prepare the Cheese Mixture:**
   - In a bowl, mix together ricotta cheese, egg, and Parmesan cheese. Set aside.
4. **Cook the Noodles:**
   - Cook lasagna noodles according to package instructions until al dente. Drain and lay flat on a parchment-lined surface to prevent sticking.
5. **Assemble the Lasagna:**
   - Spread a thin layer of meat sauce on the bottom of a 9x13-inch baking dish. Place a layer of noodles over the sauce. Spread some of the ricotta mixture over

the noodles, followed by a layer of mozzarella cheese. Repeat layers, ending with a layer of meat sauce and topping with extra mozzarella cheese.
6. **Bake:**
    - Cover with aluminum foil and bake for 25 minutes. Remove foil and bake for an additional 20 minutes, or until the cheese is bubbly and golden.
7. **Cool and Serve:**
    - Let the lasagna cool for about 10-15 minutes before cutting and serving.

Enjoy your hearty and satisfying Lasagna!

**Cornbread and Chili**

**Ingredients:**

- 1 cup all-purpose flour
- 1 cup cornmeal
- 1/4 cup granulated sugar
- 1 tablespoon baking powder
- 1/2 teaspoon salt
- 1 cup milk
- 1/4 cup vegetable oil
- 1 large egg

**Instructions:**

1. **Preheat Oven:**
   - Preheat your oven to 400°F (200°C). Grease an 8-inch square baking pan or a similar-sized skillet.
2. **Mix Dry Ingredients:**
   - In a large bowl, whisk together flour, cornmeal, sugar, baking powder, and salt.
3. **Combine Wet Ingredients:**
   - In another bowl, mix milk, vegetable oil, and egg until well combined.
4. **Combine and Bake:**
   - Stir the wet ingredients into the dry ingredients until just combined. Pour the batter into the prepared pan.
   - Bake for 20-25 minutes, or until golden brown and a toothpick inserted into the center comes out clean.
5. **Cool and Serve:**
   - Let cool slightly before cutting into squares.

## Chili

**Ingredients:**

- 2 tablespoons olive oil
- 1 pound ground beef or sausage
- 1 large onion, chopped
- 2 cloves garlic, minced
- 1 bell pepper, diced
- 1 can (14.5 ounces) diced tomatoes
- 1 can (15 ounces) kidney beans, drained and rinsed
- 1 can (15 ounces) black beans, drained and rinsed
- 1 cup beef broth
- 2 tablespoons chili powder
- 1 teaspoon ground cumin
- 1/2 teaspoon smoked paprika
- Salt and black pepper to taste

**Instructions:**

1. **Cook the Meat:**
   - Heat olive oil in a large pot over medium heat. Add ground beef or sausage and cook until browned. Drain excess fat if necessary.
2. **Sauté Vegetables:**
   - Add onion, garlic, and bell pepper to the pot. Cook until the vegetables are softened, about 5 minutes.
3. **Add Remaining Ingredients:**
   - Stir in diced tomatoes, kidney beans, black beans, beef broth, chili powder, cumin, smoked paprika, salt, and pepper. Bring to a boil.
4. **Simmer:**
   - Reduce heat and simmer for 20-30 minutes, stirring occasionally.
5. **Serve:**
   - Serve hot with cornbread on the side.

Enjoy this classic comfort food pairing!

**Chicken Tortilla Soup**

**Ingredients:**

- 2 tablespoons olive oil
- 1 large onion, chopped
- 2 cloves garlic, minced
- 1 bell pepper, diced (red or green)
- 1 can (14.5 ounces) diced tomatoes
- 4 cups chicken broth
- 1 cup cooked chicken, shredded (rotisserie chicken works well)
- 1 can (15 ounces) black beans, drained and rinsed
- 1 cup corn kernels (fresh, frozen, or canned)
- 1 teaspoon ground cumin
- 1 teaspoon chili powder
- 1/2 teaspoon paprika
- Salt and black pepper to taste
- 1-2 tablespoons lime juice (to taste)
- 1/4 cup chopped fresh cilantro (optional)

**For Serving:**

- Tortilla chips or strips
- Shredded cheddar cheese
- Sour cream
- Chopped fresh cilantro
- Lime wedges

**Instructions:**

1. **Sauté Vegetables:**
   - Heat olive oil in a large pot over medium heat. Add chopped onion and cook until softened, about 5 minutes. Stir in garlic and bell pepper, cooking for another 2-3 minutes.
2. **Add Tomatoes and Broth:**
   - Stir in diced tomatoes and chicken broth. Bring to a boil.
3. **Add Chicken and Beans:**
   - Add shredded chicken, black beans, corn, cumin, chili powder, paprika, salt, and pepper. Reduce heat and simmer for 15-20 minutes.
4. **Finish with Lime and Cilantro:**
   - Stir in lime juice and fresh cilantro if using. Adjust seasoning as needed.
5. **Serve:**
   - Ladle soup into bowls and top with tortilla chips or strips. Garnish with shredded cheese, sour cream, and additional cilantro if desired. Serve with lime wedges.

Enjoy your comforting and zesty Chicken Tortilla Soup!

**Beef and Vegetable Stew**

**Ingredients:**

- 2 tablespoons olive oil
- 1 pound beef stew meat, cut into cubes
- 1 large onion, chopped
- 2 cloves garlic, minced
- 3 carrots, sliced
- 2 celery stalks, sliced
- 1 cup potatoes, diced
- 1 cup green beans, trimmed and cut
- 4 cups beef broth
- 1 cup red wine (optional, replace with more broth if preferred)
- 1 can (14.5 ounces) diced tomatoes
- 2 tablespoons tomato paste
- 1 teaspoon dried thyme
- 1 teaspoon dried rosemary
- 1 bay leaf
- Salt and black pepper to taste
- 2 tablespoons all-purpose flour (optional, for thickening)

**Instructions:**

1. **Brown the Beef:**
   - Heat olive oil in a large pot or Dutch oven over medium-high heat. Add beef cubes and brown on all sides. Remove beef from the pot and set aside.
2. **Sauté Aromatics:**
   - In the same pot, add the onion and cook until softened, about 5 minutes. Stir in the garlic and cook for another minute.
3. **Cook Vegetables:**
   - Add carrots, celery, and potatoes to the pot. Cook for 5 minutes, stirring occasionally.
4. **Add Liquids and Seasonings:**
   - Return the browned beef to the pot. Stir in beef broth, red wine (if using), diced tomatoes, tomato paste, thyme, rosemary, and bay leaf. Bring to a boil.
5. **Simmer:**
   - Reduce heat to low, cover, and simmer for 1.5 to 2 hours, or until the beef and vegetables are tender.
6. **Thicken Stew (Optional):**
   - If you prefer a thicker stew, mix flour with a little water to create a slurry. Stir it into the stew and cook for an additional 10 minutes until thickened.
7. **Add Green Beans:**
   - Stir in green beans and cook for an additional 10 minutes until tender.
8. **Season and Serve:**
   - Remove the bay leaf. Adjust seasoning with salt and pepper to taste. Serve hot.

Enjoy your rich and comforting Beef and Vegetable Stew!

**Stuffed Acorn Squash**

**Ingredients:**

- 2 acorn squashes
- 2 tablespoons olive oil
- 1 small onion, chopped
- 2 cloves garlic, minced
- 1 cup cooked quinoa or rice
- 1/2 cup chopped pecans or walnuts
- 1/2 cup dried cranberries or raisins
- 1/2 cup shredded cheddar cheese (optional)
- 1/2 teaspoon ground cinnamon
- 1/4 teaspoon ground nutmeg
- Salt and black pepper to taste
- Fresh parsley for garnish (optional)

**Instructions:**

1. **Preheat Oven:**
   - Preheat your oven to 400°F (200°C).
2. **Prepare the Squash:**
   - Cut each acorn squash in half and scoop out the seeds. Brush the cut sides with olive oil and season with salt and pepper. Place the squash halves cut-side down on a baking sheet.
3. **Roast the Squash:**
   - Roast in the preheated oven for 25-30 minutes, or until the flesh is tender when pierced with a fork. Remove from the oven and set aside.
4. **Prepare the Filling:**
   - Heat olive oil in a skillet over medium heat. Add the chopped onion and cook until softened, about 5 minutes. Stir in the garlic and cook for another minute.
   - In a large bowl, combine the cooked quinoa or rice, chopped pecans, dried cranberries, shredded cheese (if using), cinnamon, nutmeg, salt, and pepper. Mix well.
5. **Stuff the Squash:**
   - Turn the roasted squash halves cut-side up. Spoon the filling evenly into each squash half, pressing down lightly.
6. **Bake:**
   - Return the stuffed squash to the oven and bake for an additional 10-15 minutes, until the filling is heated through and the cheese (if used) is melted.
7. **Garnish and Serve:**
   - Garnish with fresh parsley if desired. Serve warm.

Enjoy your delicious and hearty Stuffed Acorn Squash!

**Mac and Cheese Bake**

**Ingredients:**

**For the Pasta:**

- 8 ounces elbow macaroni or other short pasta
- Salt for boiling

**For the Cheese Sauce:**

- 2 tablespoons butter
- 2 tablespoons all-purpose flour
- 2 cups milk (whole milk is best)
- 1 cup heavy cream
- 2 cups shredded sharp cheddar cheese
- 1 cup shredded mozzarella cheese
- 1/2 teaspoon garlic powder
- 1/2 teaspoon onion powder
- 1/2 teaspoon mustard powder (optional)
- Salt and black pepper to taste

**For the Topping:**

- 1 cup panko breadcrumbs
- 2 tablespoons melted butter
- 1/2 cup grated Parmesan cheese
- 1 tablespoon chopped fresh parsley (optional)

**Instructions:**

1. **Preheat Oven:**
    - Preheat your oven to 375°F (190°C).
2. **Cook the Pasta:**
    - Cook the pasta in salted boiling water according to package instructions until al dente. Drain and set aside.
3. **Prepare the Cheese Sauce:**
    - In a large saucepan, melt butter over medium heat. Whisk in flour and cook for about 1 minute until lightly golden, creating a roux.
    - Gradually whisk in milk and heavy cream, cooking and stirring constantly until the mixture thickens, about 3-5 minutes.
    - Remove from heat and stir in cheddar cheese and mozzarella until melted and smooth. Season with garlic powder, onion powder, mustard powder (if using), salt, and pepper.
4. **Combine Pasta and Sauce:**
    - Add the cooked pasta to the cheese sauce, stirring until well coated.
5. **Assemble the Bake:**
    - Transfer the mac and cheese mixture to a greased 9x13-inch baking dish.
6. **Prepare the Topping:**

- In a small bowl, mix panko breadcrumbs with melted butter and grated Parmesan cheese. Sprinkle this mixture evenly over the mac and cheese.
7. **Bake:**
    - Bake in the preheated oven for 20-25 minutes, or until the topping is golden brown and the mac and cheese is bubbling.
8. **Garnish and Serve:**
    - Garnish with chopped fresh parsley if desired. Let it cool slightly before serving.

Enjoy your creamy and crispy Mac and Cheese Bake!

**Chicken Pot Roast**

**Ingredients:**

- 1 whole chicken (about 3-4 pounds), rinsed and patted dry
- 2 tablespoons olive oil
- Salt and black pepper to taste
- 1 onion, chopped
- 2 cloves garlic, minced
- 4 carrots, peeled and cut into chunks
- 3 celery stalks, cut into chunks
- 1 cup potatoes, cut into chunks
- 1 cup chicken broth
- 1/2 cup white wine (optional, replace with more broth if preferred)
- 2 tablespoons fresh thyme leaves or 1 teaspoon dried thyme
- 1 bay leaf
- 2 tablespoons all-purpose flour (optional, for thickening)
- 1 cup frozen peas (optional)

**Instructions:**

1. **Preheat Oven:**
   - Preheat your oven to 350°F (175°C).
2. **Sear the Chicken:**
   - Heat olive oil in a large ovenproof pot or Dutch oven over medium-high heat. Season the chicken with salt and pepper. Brown the chicken on all sides, about 5 minutes per side. Remove the chicken and set aside.
3. **Sauté Aromatics:**
   - In the same pot, add onion and cook until softened, about 5 minutes. Stir in garlic and cook for another minute.
4. **Add Vegetables:**
   - Add carrots, celery, and potatoes to the pot, stirring for 2-3 minutes.
5. **Add Liquids and Seasonings:**
   - Pour in chicken broth and white wine (if using). Stir in thyme and bay leaf. Return the chicken to the pot, placing it on top of the vegetables.
6. **Roast:**
   - Cover the pot with a lid and place it in the preheated oven. Roast for 1.5 to 2 hours, or until the chicken is cooked through and the vegetables are tender.
7. **Thicken the Sauce (Optional):**
   - If you prefer a thicker sauce, remove the chicken and vegetables from the pot. Stir flour into the cooking liquid, cook for 5 minutes, then return the chicken and vegetables to the pot.
8. **Add Peas (Optional):**
   - Stir in frozen peas and cook for an additional 5 minutes.
9. **Serve:**
   - Remove the bay leaf and adjust seasoning with salt and pepper as needed. Serve the chicken with vegetables and sauce.

Enjoy your comforting Chicken Pot Roast!

**Spicy Lentil Soup**

**Ingredients:**

- 2 tablespoons olive oil
- 1 large onion, chopped
- 2 cloves garlic, minced
- 2 carrots, peeled and diced
- 2 celery stalks, diced
- 1 bell pepper, diced (red or green)
- 1 cup dried brown or green lentils, rinsed and drained
- 1 can (14.5 ounces) diced tomatoes
- 6 cups vegetable or chicken broth
- 2 tablespoons tomato paste
- 1 tablespoon ground cumin
- 1 tablespoon smoked paprika
- 1 teaspoon ground coriander
- 1/2 teaspoon cayenne pepper (adjust to taste for heat)
- 1 teaspoon dried thyme
- 1 bay leaf
- Salt and black pepper to taste
- 2 cups fresh spinach or kale (optional)
- Juice of 1 lemon (optional, for brightness)

**Instructions:**

1. **Sauté Vegetables:**
   - Heat olive oil in a large pot over medium heat. Add chopped onion and cook until softened, about 5 minutes. Stir in garlic and cook for another minute.
2. **Add Carrots, Celery, and Bell Pepper:**
   - Add diced carrots, celery, and bell pepper to the pot. Cook for 5-7 minutes until vegetables start to soften.
3. **Add Spices:**
   - Stir in ground cumin, smoked paprika, ground coriander, cayenne pepper, dried thyme, and bay leaf. Cook for another 1-2 minutes until fragrant.
4. **Add Lentils and Liquids:**
   - Add the rinsed lentils, diced tomatoes, tomato paste, and broth. Bring to a boil.
5. **Simmer:**
   - Reduce heat to low, cover, and simmer for 30-40 minutes, or until lentils are tender.
6. **Add Greens (Optional):**
   - If using spinach or kale, stir them into the soup and cook for an additional 5 minutes until wilted.
7. **Season and Finish:**
   - Remove the bay leaf. Adjust seasoning with salt and pepper to taste. Stir in lemon juice if using.
8. **Serve:**

- Ladle soup into bowls and serve hot.

Enjoy your spicy and hearty Lentil Soup!

**Garlic Mashed Potatoes**

## Ingredients:

- 2 pounds potatoes (Yukon Gold or Russet), peeled and cut into chunks
- 4 cloves garlic, peeled
- 1/2 cup milk (whole milk or cream)
- 1/4 cup butter
- Salt and black pepper to taste
- Chopped fresh parsley for garnish (optional)

## Instructions:

1. **Cook Potatoes and Garlic:**
   - Place potatoes and garlic cloves in a large pot. Cover with cold water and add a pinch of salt. Bring to a boil over medium-high heat. Reduce heat and simmer until potatoes are tender, about 15-20 minutes.
2. **Drain and Mash:**
   - Drain the potatoes and garlic. Return them to the pot or a large bowl. Use a potato masher or ricer to mash until smooth.
3. **Add Milk and Butter:**
   - In a small saucepan, heat the milk and butter until the butter is melted. Gradually stir the milk mixture into the mashed potatoes until smooth and creamy. Adjust the consistency with more milk if needed.
4. **Season:**
   - Season with salt and black pepper to taste.
5. **Garnish and Serve:**
   - Garnish with chopped parsley if desired. Serve warm.

Enjoy your creamy and flavorful Garlic Mashed Potatoes!

**Seafood Chowder**

**Ingredients:**

- 2 tablespoons butter
- 1 large onion, chopped
- 2 cloves garlic, minced
- 2 celery stalks, diced
- 2 carrots, peeled and diced
- 2 cups potatoes, peeled and diced
- 4 cups seafood or chicken broth
- 1 cup heavy cream
- 1 cup milk
- 1 cup clam juice (optional, for extra flavor)
- 1 pound mixed seafood (such as shrimp, scallops, and fish fillets), cut into bite-sized pieces
- 1 cup frozen or fresh corn kernels
- 1 teaspoon dried thyme
- 1/2 teaspoon dried dill (optional)
- 1 bay leaf
- Salt and black pepper to taste
- 2 tablespoons all-purpose flour (optional, for thickening)
- Chopped fresh parsley for garnish (optional)

**Instructions:**

1. **Sauté Vegetables:**
   - In a large pot, melt butter over medium heat. Add onion, garlic, celery, and carrots. Cook until softened, about 5 minutes.
2. **Add Potatoes and Broth:**
   - Stir in diced potatoes, seafood or chicken broth, and bay leaf. Bring to a boil, then reduce heat and simmer until potatoes are tender, about 15 minutes.
3. **Add Cream and Seafood:**
   - Stir in heavy cream, milk, and clam juice (if using). Add the mixed seafood and corn. Simmer for 5-7 minutes until seafood is cooked through and corn is heated.
4. **Thicken Chowder (Optional):**
   - If you prefer a thicker chowder, mix flour with a little water to create a slurry. Stir it into the chowder and cook for an additional 5 minutes until thickened.
5. **Season:**
   - Remove the bay leaf. Stir in thyme, dill (if using), salt, and black pepper to taste.
6. **Serve:**
   - Garnish with chopped parsley if desired. Serve hot with crusty bread.

Enjoy your rich and creamy Seafood Chowder!

**Baked Chicken Parmesan**

## Ingredients:

- **4 boneless, skinless chicken breasts**
- **1 cup breadcrumbs** (preferably whole wheat or Italian-seasoned)
- **1/2 cup grated Parmesan cheese**
- **1 teaspoon dried basil**
- **1 teaspoon dried oregano**
- **1/2 teaspoon garlic powder**
- **1/2 teaspoon onion powder**
- **Salt and pepper to taste**
- **1/2 cup all-purpose flour**
- **2 large eggs, beaten**
- **1 cup marinara sauce**
- **1 cup shredded mozzarella cheese**
- **Fresh basil or parsley for garnish (optional)**

## Instructions:

1. **Preheat Oven:** Preheat your oven to 400°F (200°C). Line a baking sheet with parchment paper or lightly grease it.
2. **Prepare Chicken:** Place each chicken breast between two pieces of plastic wrap or parchment paper. Pound them to an even thickness using a meat mallet or rolling pin, about 1/2 inch thick.
3. **Prepare Breading:** In a shallow dish, mix the breadcrumbs, Parmesan cheese, dried basil, dried oregano, garlic powder, onion powder, salt, and pepper.
4. **Dredge Chicken:**
   - First, dredge each chicken breast in flour, shaking off the excess.
   - Next, dip it into the beaten eggs, allowing any excess to drip off.
   - Finally, coat the chicken in the breadcrumb mixture, pressing gently to adhere.
5. **Bake Chicken:**
   - Place the breaded chicken breasts on the prepared baking sheet.
   - Bake in the preheated oven for about 20 minutes, or until the chicken is cooked through and the internal temperature reaches 165°F (74°C).
6. **Add Sauce and Cheese:**
   - Remove the chicken from the oven. Spoon marinara sauce over each chicken breast, then sprinkle with shredded mozzarella cheese.
   - Return to the oven and bake for an additional 10 minutes, or until the cheese is melted and bubbly.
7. **Garnish and Serve:**
   - If desired, garnish with fresh basil or parsley.
   - Serve over pasta, with a side salad, or with your favorite vegetable.

Enjoy your homemade Baked Chicken Parmesan!

**Pork Schnitzel**

**Ingredients:**

- **4 boneless pork loin chops** (about 1/2 inch thick)
- **1 cup all-purpose flour**
- **2 large eggs**
- **2 tablespoons milk**
- **1 1/2 cups breadcrumbs** (preferably Italian-seasoned)
- **1/2 cup grated Parmesan cheese** (optional)
- **Salt and pepper to taste**
- **Vegetable oil** (for frying)
- **Lemon wedges** (for serving)
- **Fresh parsley** (for garnish, optional)

## Instructions:

1. **Prepare Pork Chops:**
   - Place each pork chop between two pieces of plastic wrap or parchment paper. Pound them to an even thickness using a meat mallet or rolling pin, about 1/4 inch thick. This helps ensure even cooking and a tender result.
2. **Set Up Breading Stations:**
   - In a shallow dish, place the flour. Season with salt and pepper.
   - In another shallow dish, beat the eggs with the milk.
   - In a third shallow dish, combine the breadcrumbs and Parmesan cheese, if using. Season with a little salt and pepper.
3. **Bread the Pork:**
   - Dredge each pork chop in the flour, shaking off the excess.
   - Dip into the egg mixture, allowing any excess to drip off.
   - Coat evenly with the breadcrumb mixture, pressing lightly to adhere.
4. **Heat Oil:**
   - In a large skillet, heat about 1/4 inch of vegetable oil over medium-high heat. The oil is hot enough when a breadcrumb dropped into it sizzles.
5. **Fry Schnitzels:**
   - Carefully place the breaded pork chops into the hot oil. Fry in batches if necessary to avoid overcrowding the pan.
   - Cook for about 3-4 minutes per side, or until the schnitzels are golden brown and crispy, and the internal temperature reaches 145°F (63°C).
6. **Drain and Serve:**
   - Remove the schnitzels from the skillet and place them on a paper towel-lined plate to drain any excess oil.
   - Serve hot with lemon wedges on the side. Garnish with fresh parsley if desired.

## Serving Suggestions:

- Pork Schnitzel pairs wonderfully with a side of potato salad, steamed vegetables, or a crisp green salad.

- For a traditional touch, you can also serve it with a side of lingonberry sauce or a creamy mushroom gravy.

Enjoy your homemade Pork Schnitzel!

**Creamy Chicken and Spinach Pasta**

## Ingredients:

- **12 oz (340g) pasta** (such as penne, fettuccine, or spaghetti)
- **2 tablespoons olive oil**
- **1 lb (450g) boneless, skinless chicken breasts**, cut into bite-sized pieces
- **Salt and pepper to taste**
- **1 teaspoon garlic powder**
- **1 teaspoon dried basil**
- **1 teaspoon dried oregano**
- **3 cloves garlic**, minced
- **1/2 cup onion**, finely chopped
- **1 cup heavy cream**
- **1/2 cup chicken broth**
- **1/2 cup grated Parmesan cheese**
- **2 cups fresh spinach**, roughly chopped
- **1 tablespoon lemon juice** (optional)
- **Red pepper flakes** (optional, for added heat)
- **Fresh basil or parsley** (for garnish, optional)

## Instructions:

1. **Cook Pasta:**
   - Cook the pasta according to the package instructions until al dente. Drain and set aside.
2. **Cook Chicken:**
   - In a large skillet or pan, heat the olive oil over medium heat.
   - Season the chicken pieces with salt, pepper, garlic powder, dried basil, and dried oregano.
   - Add the chicken to the skillet and cook for about 5-7 minutes, or until the chicken is cooked through and golden brown. Remove the chicken from the skillet and set aside.
3. **Prepare Sauce:**
   - In the same skillet, add a little more oil if needed and sauté the chopped onion until soft and translucent, about 3 minutes.
   - Add the minced garlic and cook for an additional 30 seconds, or until fragrant.
   - Pour in the heavy cream and chicken broth, stirring to combine. Bring to a simmer and cook for about 2-3 minutes until slightly thickened.
4. **Combine Ingredients:**
   - Reduce the heat to low and stir in the grated Parmesan cheese until melted and the sauce is smooth.
   - Add the fresh spinach and cook until wilted, about 1-2 minutes.
   - Return the cooked chicken to the skillet and stir to combine.
5. **Add Pasta:**

- Add the cooked pasta to the skillet and toss to coat the pasta evenly with the sauce. If the sauce is too thick, you can add a splash more chicken broth or a little pasta cooking water.
6. **Finish and Serve:**
    - Stir in the lemon juice if using, and adjust seasoning with more salt, pepper, or red pepper flakes as desired.
    - Garnish with fresh basil or parsley if desired.

Enjoy your creamy chicken and spinach pasta! It's perfect for a weeknight dinner or a cozy weekend meal.

**Pot Pie with Biscuits**

## Ingredients:

**For the Pot Pie Filling:**

- **2 tablespoons butter**
- **1 medium onion**, chopped
- **2 cloves garlic**, minced
- **2 carrots**, peeled and diced
- **2 celery stalks**, diced
- **1 cup frozen peas**
- **2 cups cooked chicken**, shredded or diced
- **1/4 cup all-purpose flour**
- **1 1/2 cups chicken broth**
- **1 cup milk**
- **1 teaspoon dried thyme**
- **1 teaspoon dried rosemary**
- **Salt and pepper to taste**

**For the Biscuits:**

- **2 cups all-purpose flour**
- **1 tablespoon baking powder**
- **1/2 teaspoon baking soda**
- **1/2 teaspoon salt**
- **1/2 cup cold unsalted butter**, cubed
- **3/4 cup buttermilk**

## Instructions:

1. **Prepare the Filling:**
     - In a large skillet or saucepan, melt the butter over medium heat. Add the chopped onion, garlic, carrots, and celery. Cook until the vegetables are tender, about 5 minutes.
     - Stir in the flour and cook for another 1-2 minutes, until the flour is lightly golden.
     - Gradually whisk in the chicken broth and milk, and bring to a simmer. Cook until the mixture thickens, about 5 minutes.
     - Add the peas, cooked chicken, dried thyme, dried rosemary, salt, and pepper. Stir well and remove from heat.
2. **Prepare the Biscuits:**
     - Preheat your oven to 425°F (220°C).
     - In a large bowl, whisk together the flour, baking powder, baking soda, and salt.
     - Cut in the cold butter using a pastry cutter or your fingers until the mixture resembles coarse crumbs.
     - Stir in the buttermilk until just combined. Do not overmix.
3. **Assemble and Bake:**

- Transfer the pot pie filling to a baking dish or oven-safe skillet.
- Drop spoonfuls of biscuit dough over the filling, covering it as much as possible but allowing some gaps.
- Bake in the preheated oven for 20-25 minutes, or until the biscuits are golden brown and the filling is bubbly.

4. **Serve:**
    - Let the pot pie cool slightly before serving. Enjoy this comforting dish with a side salad or as is!

This recipe combines the creamy richness of pot pie with the comforting texture of biscuits, making for a satisfying meal.

**Broccoli Cheddar Soup**

## Ingredients:

- **2 tablespoons butter**
- **1 medium onion**, chopped
- **2 cloves garlic**, minced
- **1/4 cup all-purpose flour**
- **3 cups chicken or vegetable broth**
- **2 cups milk**
- **4 cups broccoli florets**
- **1 large carrot**, peeled and diced
- **2 cups shredded cheddar cheese**
- **Salt and pepper to taste**
- **1/2 teaspoon dried thyme** (optional)
- **1/4 teaspoon paprika** (optional)

## Instructions:

1. **Sauté Vegetables:**
   - In a large pot, melt the butter over medium heat. Add the chopped onion and cook until soft, about 4-5 minutes.
   - Add the minced garlic and cook for another 1 minute until fragrant.
2. **Make Roux:**
   - Stir in the flour and cook for 1-2 minutes, until lightly golden, to form a roux.
3. **Add Broth and Milk:**
   - Gradually whisk in the broth and milk, ensuring there are no lumps. Bring to a simmer and cook until slightly thickened, about 5 minutes.
4. **Cook Vegetables:**
   - Add the broccoli florets and diced carrot to the pot. Simmer until the vegetables are tender, about 10-15 minutes.
5. **Blend Soup (optional):**
   - For a smoother texture, use an immersion blender to partially blend the soup, or carefully transfer some of it to a blender and blend in batches. Leave some chunks for texture if desired.
6. **Add Cheese:**
   - Stir in the shredded cheddar cheese until melted and smooth. Season with salt, pepper, dried thyme, and paprika if using.
7. **Serve:**
   - Ladle the soup into bowls and enjoy with crusty bread or a side salad.

This creamy, cheesy soup is perfect for a cozy meal!


**Sausage and Kale Soup**

## Ingredients:

- **2 tablespoons olive oil**
- **1 lb (450g) Italian sausage**, casing removed
- **1 medium onion**, chopped
- **3 cloves garlic**, minced
- **3 carrots**, peeled and sliced
- **2 celery stalks**, chopped
- **6 cups chicken or vegetable broth**
- **2 cups potatoes**, diced
- **1 bunch kale**, stems removed and leaves chopped
- **1 teaspoon dried thyme**
- **1/2 teaspoon dried rosemary**
- **Salt and pepper to taste**

## Instructions:

1. **Cook Sausage:**
   - In a large pot, heat the olive oil over medium heat. Add the sausage and cook, breaking it up with a spoon, until browned and cooked through. Remove the sausage with a slotted spoon and set aside.
2. **Sauté Vegetables:**
   - In the same pot, add the chopped onion, garlic, carrots, and celery. Cook until the vegetables are softened, about 5-7 minutes.
3. **Add Broth and Potatoes:**
   - Stir in the chicken or vegetable broth and diced potatoes. Bring to a boil, then reduce heat and simmer until the potatoes are tender, about 10-15 minutes.
4. **Add Kale and Sausage:**
   - Stir in the chopped kale and cooked sausage. Cook until the kale is wilted and tender, about 5 minutes.
5. **Season and Serve:**
   - Add dried thyme, dried rosemary, salt, and pepper to taste. Adjust seasoning as needed.
   - Serve hot with crusty bread or a side salad.

Enjoy this warm and nourishing soup!

**Chicken and Dumplings**

## Ingredients:

**For the Chicken Stew:**

- **2 tablespoons olive oil**
- **1 lb (450g) boneless, skinless chicken breasts or thighs**, diced
- **1 medium onion**, chopped
- **2 cloves garlic**, minced
- **3 carrots**, peeled and diced
- **2 celery stalks**, diced
- **4 cups chicken broth**
- **1 cup milk**
- **1 cup frozen peas**
- **1/4 cup all-purpose flour**
- **1 teaspoon dried thyme**
- **1/2 teaspoon dried rosemary**
- **Salt and pepper to taste**

**For the Dumplings:**

- **1 1/2 cups all-purpose flour**
- **2 teaspoons baking powder**
- **1/2 teaspoon baking soda**
- **1/2 teaspoon salt**
- **1/4 cup cold unsalted butter**, cubed
- **3/4 cup buttermilk**

## Instructions:

1. **Prepare the Chicken Stew:**
   - In a large pot, heat olive oil over medium heat. Add diced chicken and cook until browned and cooked through. Remove chicken and set aside.
   - In the same pot, add onion, garlic, carrots, and celery. Cook until vegetables are softened, about 5-7 minutes.
   - Stir in flour and cook for 1-2 minutes. Gradually whisk in chicken broth and milk. Bring to a simmer and cook until slightly thickened, about 5 minutes.
   - Add peas, cooked chicken, dried thyme, dried rosemary, salt, and pepper. Stir to combine and keep warm.
2. **Make the Dumplings:**
   - In a bowl, whisk together flour, baking powder, baking soda, and salt. Cut in cold butter until the mixture resembles coarse crumbs. Stir in buttermilk until just combined.
3. **Cook the Dumplings:**

- Drop spoonfuls of dumpling dough onto the simmering stew. Cover the pot with a lid and cook for 15-20 minutes, or until the dumplings are cooked through and fluffy. Do not lift the lid while cooking.
4. **Serve:**
    - Ladle the stew and dumplings into bowls and serve hot.

Enjoy this cozy, hearty meal!

**Beef Meatballs in Marinara**

## Ingredients:

**For the Meatballs:**

- 1 lb (450g) ground beef
- 1/2 cup breadcrumbs
- 1/4 cup grated Parmesan cheese
- 1/4 cup fresh parsley, chopped (or 1 tablespoon dried parsley)
- 1 large egg
- 2 cloves garlic, minced
- 1 teaspoon dried oregano
- 1/2 teaspoon dried basil
- Salt and pepper to taste

**For the Marinara Sauce:**

- 2 tablespoons olive oil
- 1 medium onion, chopped
- 3 cloves garlic, minced
- 1 (28-ounce) can crushed tomatoes
- 2 tablespoons tomato paste
- 1 teaspoon dried oregano
- 1 teaspoon dried basil
- 1/2 teaspoon sugar (optional, to taste)
- Salt and pepper to taste

## Instructions:

1. **Prepare the Meatballs:**
   - Preheat your oven to 375°F (190°C) and line a baking sheet with parchment paper or lightly grease it.
   - In a large bowl, combine the ground beef, breadcrumbs, Parmesan cheese, parsley, egg, minced garlic, dried oregano, dried basil, salt, and pepper. Mix until just combined; don't overmix.
   - Shape the mixture into meatballs, about 1 to 1.5 inches in diameter, and place them on the prepared baking sheet.
2. **Bake the Meatballs:**
   - Bake in the preheated oven for about 20 minutes, or until the meatballs are cooked through and have an internal temperature of 160°F (71°C). Remove from the oven and set aside.
3. **Prepare the Marinara Sauce:**
   - While the meatballs are baking, heat olive oil in a large skillet or saucepan over medium heat.

- Add the chopped onion and cook until softened and translucent, about 5 minutes.
- Add the minced garlic and cook for an additional 1 minute, until fragrant.
- Stir in the crushed tomatoes, tomato paste, dried oregano, dried basil, and sugar (if using). Bring to a simmer and cook for about 10-15 minutes, allowing the flavors to meld. Season with salt and pepper to taste.

4. **Combine Meatballs and Sauce:**
    - Once the meatballs are baked, add them to the marinara sauce. Simmer the meatballs in the sauce for an additional 10 minutes to let the flavors blend.
5. **Serve:**
    - Serve the meatballs and marinara sauce over pasta, in a sub roll for a meatball sandwich, or with a side of garlic bread. Garnish with extra Parmesan cheese and fresh basil or parsley if desired.

Enjoy your homemade Beef Meatballs in Marinara!

**Creamy Shrimp and Grits**

## Ingredients:

**For the Grits:**

- **1 cup stone-ground grits**
- **4 cups water or chicken broth**
- **1 cup milk**
- **1/2 cup grated Parmesan cheese**
- **2 tablespoons butter**
- **Salt and pepper to taste**

**For the Shrimp:**

- **1 lb (450g) large shrimp**, peeled and deveined
- **2 tablespoons olive oil**
- **1/2 cup onion**, finely chopped
- **3 cloves garlic**, minced
- **1/2 cup chicken broth**
- **1/4 cup heavy cream**
- **1 tablespoon lemon juice**
- **1 teaspoon smoked paprika**
- **1/2 teaspoon dried thyme**
- **Salt and pepper to taste**
- **2 tablespoons fresh parsley**, chopped (for garnish)

## Instructions:

1. **Prepare the Grits:**
    - In a large pot, bring the water or chicken broth to a boil.
    - Gradually whisk in the grits, reducing heat to low. Cover and cook, stirring occasionally, until the grits are tender and thickened, about 20-25 minutes.
    - Stir in the milk, Parmesan cheese, and butter. Season with salt and pepper to taste. Keep warm while you prepare the shrimp.
2. **Cook the Shrimp:**
    - In a large skillet, heat olive oil over medium heat. Add the chopped onion and cook until softened, about 3-4 minutes.
    - Add the minced garlic and cook for an additional 1 minute, until fragrant.
    - Add the shrimp to the skillet and cook until pink and opaque, about 2-3 minutes per side.
    - Remove the shrimp from the skillet and set aside.
3. **Make the Sauce:**

- In the same skillet, add chicken broth, heavy cream, lemon juice, smoked paprika, and dried thyme. Bring to a simmer and cook until the sauce is slightly thickened, about 3-4 minutes.
- Return the cooked shrimp to the skillet and toss to coat in the sauce. Cook for an additional 2 minutes to heat through.

4. **Serve:**
    - Spoon the creamy grits onto plates or into bowls.
    - Top with the shrimp and sauce.
    - Garnish with fresh parsley and serve.

Enjoy your delicious and creamy Shrimp and Grits!

www.ingramcontent.com/pod-product-compliance
Lightning Source LLC
LaVergne TN
LVHW081618060526
838201LV00054B/2301